To my little
with a lotte

Happy Christmas —
this is to fill the hours
when you've got "nothing to do"!!
Duff & Dana X X

FRANCIS FRITH'S
PHOTOGRAPHIC MEMORIES

SUFFOLK

A SECOND SELECTION

CLIVE PAINE was born and educated in Bury St Edmunds, and apart from his years at university, has worked there all his life. He is a teacher, lecturer, author and broadcaster on all aspects of local history. He has taught history and local history for nearly 30 years, 21 of which have been as County Advisory Teacher for Archives and Local History in Suffolk. He frequently broadcasts on local and national radio, and appeared with Prince Edward on his 'Crown and Country' series for ITV; he has also been profiled in 'Reader's Digest'. He is a Council member of the Suffolk Institute of Archaeology and History, the executive of the Suffolk Local History Council, and past Chairman of the Education Committee of the British Association for Local History. He is also a Lay Reader at St Mary's in Bury.

FRANCIS FRITH'S
PHOTOGRAPHIC MEMORIES

SUFFOLK
A SECOND SELECTION
PHOTOGRAPHIC MEMORIES

CLIVE PAINE

First published in the United Kingdom in 2003 by
Frith Book Company Ltd

Paperback Edition 2003
ISBN 1-85937-458-1

British Library Cataloguing in Publication Data

Francis Frith's Suffolk - A Second Selection
Clive Paine

Frith Book Company Ltd
Frith's Barn, Teffont,
Salisbury, Wiltshire SP3 5QP
Tel: +44 (0) 1722 716 376
Email: info@francisfrith.co.uk
www.francisfrith.co.uk

Printed and bound in Great Britain

Front Cover: **WOODBRIDGE,** *The Beach 1898* 42773
Title Page: **NEWMARKET,** *1922* 71917

AS WITH ANY HISTORICAL DATABASE THE FRITH ARCHIVE IS CONSTANTLY
BEING CORRECTED AND IMPROVED AND THE PUBLISHERS WOULD
WELCOME INFORMATION ON OMISSIONS OR INACCURACIES.

Acknowledgements

In preparing the captions I have visited each one of the locations and met so many
generous people who helped me with their local knowledge and memories. I wish
especially to thank the following for their essential contributions to the book:
Sue Andrews, Sheila Gooch, Martin Harrison, Joyce Hazelwood, Michael Horne,
Bob Malster, David Page, Stephanie Palmer, Angela Plumb, Ann Pryke, Jack Raynham,
Jennie Robinson, Ernest Shaw, Mel Spurling, Jack and Jill Stiff, Robert Webster,
Liz Wigmore and Steve Williams. Many thanks also go to Jane Cummins, who brilliantly
deciphered my handwriting to set the text, and to David Caruth, who read the proofs.
Any mistakes in matter of detail are of course mine alone.

CONTENTS

FRANCIS FRITH
VICTORIAN PIONEER

FRANCIS FRITH, founder of the world-famous photographic archive, was a complex and multi-talented man. A devout Quaker and a highly successful Victorian businessman, he was philosophic by nature and pioneering in outlook.

By 1855 he had already established a wholesale grocery business in Liverpool, and sold it for the astonishing sum of £200,000, which is the equivalent today of over £15,000,000. Now a multi-millionaire, he was able to indulge his passion for travel. As a child he had pored over travel books written by early explorers, and his fancy and imagination had been stirred by family holidays to the sublime mountain regions of Wales and Scotland. 'What a land of spirit-stirring and enriching scenes and places!' he had written. He was to return to these scenes of grandeur in later years to 'recapture the thousands of vivid and tender memories', but with a different purpose. Now in his thirties, and captivated by the new science of photography, Frith set out on a series of pioneering journeys up the Nile and to the

Near East that occupied him from 1856 until 1860.

INTRIGUE AND EXPLORATION

These far-flung journeys were packed with intrigue and adventure. In his life story, written when he was sixty-three, Frith tells of being held captive by bandits, and of fighting 'an awful midnight battle to the very point of surrender with a deadly pack of hungry, wild dogs'. Wearing flowing Arab costume, Frith arrived at Akaba by camel seventy years before Lawrence of Arabia, where he encountered 'desert princes and rival sheikhs, blazing with jewel-hilted swords'.

He was the first photographer to venture beyond the sixth cataract of the Nile. Africa was still the mysterious 'Dark Continent', and Stanley and Livingstone's historic meeting was a decade into the future. The conditions for picture taking confound belief. He laboured for hours in his wicker dark-room in the sweltering heat of the desert, while the volatile chemicals fizzed dangerously in their trays. Back in London he exhibited his photographs and was 'rapturously cheered' by members of the Royal Society. His reputation as a photographer was made overnight.

VENTURE OF A LIFE-TIME

Characteristically, Frith quickly spotted the opportunity to create a new business as a specialist publisher of photographs. He lived in an era of immense and sometimes violent change.

For the poor, in the early part of Victoria's reign, work was exhausting and the hours long, and people had precious little free time to enjoy themselves. Most had no transport other than a cart or gig at their disposal, and rarely travelled far beyond the boundaries of their own town or village. However, by the 1870s the railways had threaded their way across the country, and Bank Holidays and half-day Saturdays had been made obligatory by Act of Parliament. All of a sudden the working man and his family were able to enjoy days out and see a little more of the world.

With typical business acumen, Francis Frith foresaw that these new tourists would enjoy having souvenirs to commemorate their days out. In 1860 he married Mary Ann Rosling and set out on a new career: his aim was to photograph every city, town and village in Britain. For the next thirty years he travelled the country by train and by pony and trap, producing fine photographs of seaside resorts and beauty spots that were keenly bought by millions of Victorians. These prints were painstakingly pasted into family albums and pored over during the dark nights of winter, rekindling precious memories of summer excursions.

THE RISE OF FRITH & CO

Frith's studio was soon supplying retail shops all over the country. To meet the demand he gath-

ered about him a small team of photographers, and published the work of independent artist-photographers of the calibre of Roger Fenton and Francis Bedford. In order to gain some understanding of the scale of Frith's business one only has to look at the catalogue issued by Frith & Co in 1886: it runs to some 670 pages, listing not only many thousands of views of the British Isles but also many photographs of most European countries, and China, Japan, the USA and Canada - note the sample page shown here from the hand-written Frith & Co ledgers recording the pictures. By 1890 Frith had created the greatest specialist photographic publishing company in the world, with over 2,000 sales outlets - more than the combined number that Boots and WH Smith have today! The picture on the next page shows the Frith & Co display board at Ingleton in the Yorkshire Dales. Beautifully constructed with mahogany frame and gilt inserts, it could display up to a dozen local scenes.

POSTCARD BONANZA

The ever-popular holiday postcard we know today took many years to develop. In 1870 the Post Office issued the first plain cards, with a pre-printed stamp on one face. In 1894 they allowed other publishers' cards to be sent through the mail with an attached adhesive half-penny stamp. Demand grew rapidly, and in 1895 a new size of postcard was permitted called the court card, but there was little room for illustration. In 1899, a year after Frith's death, a new card measuring 5.5 x 3.5 inches became the standard format, but it was not until 1902 that the divided back came into being, so that the address and message could be on one face and a full-size illustration on the other. Frith & Co were in the vanguard of postcard development: Frith's sons Eustace and Cyril continued their father's monumental task, expanding the number of views offered to the public and recording more

and more places in Britain, as the coasts and countryside were opened up to mass travel.

Francis Frith had died in 1898 at his villa in Cannes, his great project still growing. The archive he created continued in business for another seventy years. By 1970 it contained over a third of a million pictures showing 7,000 British towns and villages.

FRANCIS FRITH'S LEGACY

Frith's legacy to us today is of immense significance and value, for the magnificent archive of evocative photographs he created provides a unique record of change in the cities, towns and villages throughout Britain over a century and more. Frith and his fellow studio photographers revisited locations many times down the years to update their views, compiling for us an enthralling and colourful pageant of British life and character.

We are fortunate that Frith was dedicated to recording the minutiae of everyday life. For it is this sheer wealth of visual data, the painstaking chronicle of changes in dress, transport, street layouts, buildings, housing, engineering and landscape that captivates us so much today. His remarkable images offer us a powerful link with the past and with the lives of our ancestors.

THE VALUE OF THE ARCHIVE TODAY

Computers have now made it possible for Frith's many thousands of images to be accessed almost instantly. Frith's images are increasingly used as visual resources, by social historians, by researchers into genealogy and ancestry, by architects and town planners, and by teachers involved in local history projects.

In addition, the archive offers every one of us an opportunity to examine the places where we and our families have lived and worked down the years. Highly successful in Frith's own era, the archive is now, a century and more on, entering a new phase of popularity. Historians consider the Francis Frith Collection to be of prime national importance. It is the only archive of its kind remaining in private ownership. Francis Frith's archive is now housed in an historic timber barn in the beautiful village of Teffont in Wiltshire. Its founder would not recognize the archive office as it is today. In place of the many thousands of dusty boxes containing glass plate negatives and an all-pervading odour of photographic chemicals, there are now ranks of computer screens. He would be amazed to watch his images travelling round the world at unimaginable speeds through internet lines.

The archive's future is both bright and exciting. Francis Frith, with his unshakeable belief in making photographs available to the greatest number of people, would undoubtedly approve of what is being done today with his lifetime's work. His photographs depicting our shared past are now bringing pleasure and enlightenment to millions around the world a century and more after his death.

SUFFOLK
AN INTRODUCTION

THE photographs of Suffolk in this second selection cover the period between the 1890s and the early 1960s. Included here are views of the castles, monastic remains, churches, manor houses, individual buildings, houses of timber, plaster and brick, towns, villages, seaside resorts and ports, rivers and coastline that contribute to the unique Suffolk landscape.

Suffolk is bounded by the River Waveney on the north and the River Stour on the south. In between, to the east, are the coastal towns and villages such as Lowestoft, Southwold, Walberswick, Dunwich, Aldeburgh, Orford, Bawdsey and Felixstowe. There are also river estuaries: Aldeburgh lies on the Ald; Bawdsey, Waldringfield, Woodbridge and Melton lie on the Deben; and Trimley, Pin Mill, Woolverstone and Ipswich lie on the Orwell.

In the medieval period, Suffolk was divided into three areas. The Liberty of St Edmund was centred on Bury, and the Liberty of St Etheldreda on Woodbridge; the area between, called the

Geldable, was administered from Beccles and Ipswich. In 1889 Suffolk became two counties: the Liberty of St Edmund became West Suffolk and the two other areas became East Suffolk. This division lasted until 1974, when Ipswich became the capital, although Bury retained its role as an administrative centre.

Until 1914 Suffolk was part of the Diocese of Norwich and Ely. It then became the Diocese of St Edmundsbury and Ipswich, so named because the cathedral was in Bury (the former St James's church) and the bishop lived in Ipswich.

Throughout the period 1890-1960, Suffolk remained a predominantly agricultural county. In 1891 there were only six towns and in 1961 only eight with populations over 6,000, making up only 30% and 52% of the total population of the county. Ipswich was the largest town, with a population of 56,000 in 1891 and 117,000 in 1961; Lowestoft's was 19,000 rising to 45,000; and Bury's was 16,000 rising to 21,000. At fourth place in 1891 was Beccles with 6,000, supplanted by Felixstowe in 1961 with 17,000 people.

From c1880, except for the First World War, agriculture was in a depressed state, caused mainly by the importation of cheap foods. The effect of this was the closure of village shops, craftsmen going out of business and younger people migrating to other parts of the county or emigrating to other parts of the Empire. Housing was poor: the now much-desired timber-framed and thatched cottages were in a very different condition before the restorations and conversions of more recent times. However, the first rural council houses in the country were built at Ixworth in 1893. The earliest post-war urban council houses were at Bury St Edmunds in 1919 and Ipswich in 1920. Agriculture revived from 1939 onwards; farm sizes increased, and a variety of machinery replaced horses, whose

numbers fell by 91% between 1911 and 1958.

In most rural areas in the 1940s, water still came from wells; there was neither sewerage nor electricity - the privy and the oil lamp were common. However, most towns had piped water, sewerage and electricity. In 1951, 28% of Suffolk homes were without piped water, 34% were without WCs and 53% were without fixed baths. By 1971, all had piped water; only 4% were without WCs and 11% without baths.

The vast majority of parishes still had a resident clergyman at the rectory or vicarage. The village school, usually dating from the Victorian period, was still open and educating successive generations of children. The village shops, including the post office, served the needs of the locals without the threat of competition from supermarkets. The village pubs, in the days before pub food, carpets and muzak, provided real ale, traditional entertainment and a sense of community. The photographs show shops, post offices, Co-operative stores, butchers, bakers, blacksmiths, drapers, grocers, pubs, hotels and a wider variety of shops in the towns.

The greatest changes in Suffolk were to come later. These were mainly losses, including the loss of railway links in the Beeching cuts after 1963; of village shops thanks to the supermarkets; of village schools due to the declining child population; of pubs due to the closure and amalgamation of breweries; and of village crafts, as their need and use abated. Growth came with the influx of overspill from London to new estates, and with the popularity of East Anglia as a place of second homes and retirement.

The photographs record some of the historic sites of Suffolk, such as the two outstandingly important castles of Orford and Framlingham. Orford, built 1165-73, was the first English castle to be built with a circular faceted keep with towers. Framingham, built 1190-1210, was the first to be built without a keep, but with a fortified curtain wall, strengthened with 13 towers. In both these places, and at Bungay, Eye and Clare, the outline of the castle bailey and ditches affected the plan of the adjacent town, with curving streets, the market place near the castle gate, and the church nearby. It was at Framlingham in 1553 that Princess Mary Tudor rallied the people of Norfolk and Suffolk, who helped her reclaim the crown from Lady Jane Grey.

Before the Dissolution of 1535-39, Suffolk had a large number of abbeys, priories, friaries and nunneries. This gave rise to the term 'Selig Suffolk' (meaning 'holy', not 'silly'). The second largest Benedictine abbey in the country was built at Bury St Edmunds to house the remains of St Edmund, king of East Anglia, who died at Bradfield St Clare in 689. The abbey church was 50 feet larger than the Norwich Cathedral, but very little of the building remains today, except for the magnificent gateways. Smaller religious sites at Dunwich, Leiston and Butley are included in this collection, and so is Friars Street in Sudbury, whose name is a reminder of a religious foundation.

In the medieval period every parish had its church, most of which had been recorded in 1086 in the Domesday Book. Many of the churches were rebuilt in the 15th century as a thanksgiving for new-found wealth. Some of this wealth derived from the cloth trade, such as Lavenham, Long Melford, Clare and Cavendish; some from coastal and river trade, such as Beccles, Bungay, Southwold, Blythburgh, East Bergholt and Mildenhall; and some from the commerce of administrative and market centres, such as Framingham, Eye, Wickham Market,

Needham Market, Stowmarket and Sudbury.

In this collection, churches form the backdrop to over half the photographs. The churches are in a commanding position in the community, and are mainly built of the local flint, which was also used in the flushwork decoration on the parapets, buttresses and towers. The few churches that are built of stone, which was brought into Suffolk from Rutland and Northamptonshire, are those with the greatest expenditure lavished upon them.

Suffolk was a county of landed estates. In 1888, 39% of the land was owned by 38 people and nearly 60% of the land was in estates of over 1,000 acres. Many of these estates were sold between the wars; many of the houses that they served were demolished between 1920 and the 1960s. Photographs of Kentwell, Christchurch and Somerleyton show large houses of the Tudor and Jacobean periods. Woolverstone is a Georgian mansion overlooking the River Orwell. Bawdsey, on the coast, is a Victorian and Edwardian fantasy, with a tower added for every million pounds its owner made on the stock market. Representing the humbler buildings on an estate is the thatched entrance lodge at Great Barton.

The medieval and Tudor timber-framed jettied houses in Suffolk towns and villages are as much part of the landscape as the trees from which they were constructed. In the 18th century many houses were refronted in plaster or brick, to give them a more modern appearance. From the 1960s onwards the trend developed (now mainly halted) of exposing the whole timber framing, revealing far more than was intended by their original builders. The photographs of town and village streets all include timber and refronted timber buildings, but none is surpassed by Kersey, Lavenham, Long Melford, Hartest, Clare and Cavendish in the south-west corner of the county.

Brick has been used as a local building material since the 15th century, and very widely in the 18th and 19th centuries. There are excellent examples of brick refronting or houses built of brick at Lowestoft, Beccles, Kessingland, Southwold, Framlingham, Orford, Ipswich, Woolpit, Sudbury and Haverhill.

Most of the industries and crafts of Suffolk were adjuncts to the two main spheres of agriculture and fishing. Agricultural machinery was produced by Garrett's of Leiston, Smythe's of Peasenhall, Ransomes Sims & Jefferies of Ipswich, and Boby's of Bury St Edmunds. Between them these firms made steam engines, steam and horse-drawn ploughs, seed drills and threshing machines.

In 1900, there were maltings in 13% of Suffolk parishes, and can be seen today at Woodbridge and Stowmarket. Since Domesday, water power (and wind power since the 13th century) has been harnessed to drive mills. Later examples of watermills are shown in this book at Wickham Market, Needham Market, Ixworth and Barton Mills; we can also see a post windmill at Holton and a tower mill at Pakenham. Stowmarket's wide range of industries along the River Gipping is represented by the tannery.

Along the coast, the photographs record the various towns and villages which have become seaside retreats and resorts. Southwold, Aldeburgh and Lowestoft had long been famed for the curative powers of sea bathing. Lowestoft was developed by Sir Samuel Morton Peto in the 1840s and 1850s and Felixstowe by Colonel George Tomline in the 1870s. They both built houses for residents and visitors; built a railway to bring in trade and tourists; and created docks and harbours to bring trade and employment. Lowestoft was described in 1886 as 'the very pink of propriety'. Felixstowe, following the visit of the German Empress in 1891, was known as 'The Queen of the East Coast Resorts'.

The areas of Southwold, Walberswick and Aldeburgh photographed here have changed very little, and remain genteel, cultured and almost timeless. Walberswick, in the late Victorian and Edwardian period, was the home of a colony of artists, including Philip Street and Charles Rennie Mackintosh. Aldeburgh is now the home of the annual Festival started in 1948 by Benjamin Britten. Dunwich is famous for fish and chips and disappearing into the sea. Thorpeness is another purpose-built seaside village in the tiny hamlet of Thorpe in Aldringham. It was built 1910-28 as a 'Garden Village and model holiday hamlet by the sea'. This timber-framed black and white Tudor fantasy was the creation of Glencain Stuart Ogilvie of Sizewell Hall.

Suffolk is the home of two major artists. Thomas Gainsborough (1727-88) was born at Sudbury. He lived in Friars Street from 1748 to 1752; here two of his daughters were born - they were painted in 'The Artist's Daughters Chasing a Butterfly' (1756). John Constable (1776-1837) was born at East Bergholt. The villages along the Stour valley between Nayland and Flatford are known as Constable Country, where his churches, rivers, landscapes, clouds and vast sky all remain to be seen today.

The photographs in this second selection of Suffolk are arranged as a tour of the county, based on the District Council areas established in 1974.

LOWESTOFT
AND WAVENEY

FRITTON DECOY
From the Parlor 1890 24034

Fritton Lake, like the Broads, originated as a series of
peat pits in the medieval period. It was later used as a
duck decoy. The ducks were drawn into the decoy by
the decoy man's dog. Their natural curiosity led them
to their death at the end of the funnel-like decoy pipe,
whose entrance is to the right of the boathouse on the
opposite bank.

SOMERLEYTON
Somerleyton Hall
1891 28726

Somerleyton was built 1844-51 by Sir Samuel Morton Peto, the railway contractor, builder and developer of Lowestoft. The building was designed by John Thomas (who had worked with Peto on the new Houses of Parliament) in the Jacobean style, incorporating the existing house. Pevsner described the Hall as 'more Jacobean than any original Jacobean house'.

SOMERLEYTON, *Somerleyton Hall, the Winter Garden 1891* 28729

The Winter Garden was a miniature Crystal Palace, 126 feet by 136 feet, with glazed arcades and a domed glass roof. The fountain and statue in the fernery (centre) was made by Joseph Durham in 1868. Under-floor heating allowed tropical and exotic plants to be grown in beds, whilst climbing greenery smothered the pillars and roof. Most of the structure was demolished in 1914, but a small section and some statues survive.

◄ **OULTON BROAD**
Hoisting Sail c1955
O30053

The yacht is passing by the north side of the Broad, with 1930s bungalows along the frontage. The yacht is typical of those developed since the 1930s for use on the Broads. The three men are tightening up the burgee. The two girls are wearing knitted hats, an essential part of post-war dress.

◄**OULTON BROAD** *1887*
19876

Oulton was another of the series of medieval broads stretching northward into Norfolk. Here are three yachts typical of the period, as there was then little difference between those used on the sea or the Broads. However, it seems that one is stuck with its keel in the mud. The man in the rowing boat appears to be getting ready to pull the yacht off.

▲ **LOWESTOFT,** *The Lighthouse and the Cottages 1887* 19849

Between the High Street and the Beach village, where the fishing community lived, were 12 narrow alleys, known as Scores. This row of fishermen's cottages took their name from the High Light, the lighthouse we can see in the background. The dioptric light was lit by oil until 1938, when it was electrified. The cottages were demolished the same year and replaced by council houses.

◄**LOWESTOFT**
The Esplanade 1887
19831

South Lowestoft was developed in the 1840s and 1850s by Sir Samuel Morton Peto. The Esplanade had semi-detached villas and Bath-style terraces for the upper and middle classes, designed by John Thomas. We are looking north from Parade Road to the south pier of the Outer Harbour, begun in 1846. The statue is one of a pair of tritons. They are holding cornucopias, which is unusual - they indicate the bounty Peto would gain from his speculation.

LOWESTOFT
*Claremont Pier from
Kirkley Cliff 1921* 71693

The pier was built in 1903
by the Coastal Development
Company to enable visitors
to arrive by Belle steamers -
the company ran a service
between London and
Yarmouth. To the left are the
'second-class' houses of
Marine Parade, the spire of
St John's church, built in
1853, and the 'first-class'
houses of the Esplanade.

▼ **LOWESTOFT,** *Wellington Gardens 1921* 71697

These gardens lay north of Claremont Pier and in front of Wellington Esplanade, on the left. In 1925 the area was described as 'lined with houses of a superior character, many of which are retained by county families for summer occupation'. The gardens were provided with ornamental ponds and a central shelter. In Claremont Road either the cabby or his fare wait patiently.

► **LOWESTOFT**
A Trip in the Lifeboat
c1950 L105006

The Hatfield Hotel (centre right) looks very modern for 1950, and contrasts with the Victorian buildings on Parade Road South. In the foreground is a Victorian sprung cart in the shape of a lifeboat. The little girl, strapped in for safety and concentrating on hanging on, looks much more Victorian than post-war, and should be in the Lifeboat Day Parade.

◀ **LOWESTOFT**
*View from
Pakefield 1890*
24022

The timber building with steps leading down from the cliff (right) is the Pakefield lifeboat shed, which was washed away by 1905. The Ordnance Survey maps of 1884 and 1905 show a massive loss of coastline along the cliff. The lifeboat was called the 'Two Sisters, Mary and Hannah'; she was built at Lowestoft and was in service 1872-1910. The fishermen relax on the cliff top, whilst their boats are drawn up on the beach.

▶ **BECCLES**
Market Place 1894
33334

The tall brick building was Thomas Self, greengrocer and market gardener; to the left was Clement Poll, butcher. The shorter building, now a bookshop, has since been heightened to match the adjacent rooflines. To the right of Self's is William Loades, ironmonger, with cycles and other items displayed on the pavement. The ironmonger's has been rebuilt and Self's altered since 1894.

BECCLES
Antique Trail

N

TO NORWICH ← ○ A146 → TO LOWESTOFT

TO THE QUAY

SALTGATE

SMALLGATE

NEWGATE

THE WALK

NEW MARKET

MARKET ST

STATION ROAD

RAILWAY STATION

NEWGATE

HUNGATE LANE

HUNGATE

BLYBURGATE

TO BUNGAY
B1062

PEDDARS LANE

LONDON ROAD

TO WORLINGHAM/ LOWESTOFT →

INGATE

ELLOUGH RD

TO IPSWICH
A145

❶ Blyburgate Antiques
❷ Eclectics
❸ Durrants Auction Rooms
❹ Plaice Antiques
❺ Fauconberges
❻ One Step Back
❼ Pynappel Antiekes
❽ Vintage Mischief
Further details on reverse
SAT NAV: NR34
P Parking
⚠ Toilets

❶ Blyburgate Antiques

Family owned antique shop selling a wide variety of good quality antiques and collectables; china, jewellery, silver, glass, metalware, furniture, postcards etc.

Probate, insurance and house clearances also undertaken

27-29 Blyburgate, NR34 9TB
Tel: 01502 711174
email: kates.lee@virgin.net
Open Tues, Thurs-Sat 10 - 4pm

❷ Eclectics

Selection of original fireplaces, antiques and collectables inc: furniture, garden statuary and lighting

1 Ingate, NR34 9RU
Tel: 01502 719709
or 07811 350995
Open Tues - Sat 10 - 5pm
Sun & Bank Holidays 11- 4
email: eclecticsbeccles@aol.com

❸ Durrants Auction Rooms

Professional auctioneers and valuers of antiques and collectables. Formal valuations for all purposes and house clearances undertaken.

The Old School House,
Peddars Lane, NR34 9UE
Tel: 01502 713490
email: auctionrooms@durrants.com
www.durrants.com
Live bidding: www.the-saleroon.com/durrants
Open Mon- Fri 9am - 4.30pm and Sat after sales 9am - 12pm

❹ Plaice Antiques

Unusual items bought and sold and always in stock

25 Blyburgate, NR34 9TB
Tel 01502 713151
Open Thurs - Sat 9.30-4pm

❺ Fauconberges

Buying and selling traditional English Antiques in Beccles since 1976

Probate, family division and insurance valuations, house clearances and contents dispersal discretely conducted.

8 Smallgate, NR34 9AD
Tel: 01502 716147
Open Monday 1pm - 4pm
Tues, Thurs, Fri, Sat 10.30am - 4pm
Closed All Day Wednesday

❻ One Step Back

*Furniture, etc
Antique & Design*

For all the things that make a home

2 Exchange Square, NR34 9HL
Tel: 01502 714121
Open Mon - Sat 10-5pm
Closed Weds
email: dianewells@btconnect.com

❼ Pynappel Antiekes

European sourced antique furniture, ceramics, artwork and any other interesting bits seen. Dutch Delftware and other European earthenware a particular speciality.

2 Saltgate, NR34 9AN
Tel 07957 225297
email dave@pynappel.com
www.pynappel.com
Open Weds - Sat 10-4pm

❽ Vintage Mischief

*Blending art, mid-century furniture, fashion, ceramics and jewellery.
Items purchases*

The Old Dairy, Hungate Lane,
NR34 9TN
Tel 07596050868
email: info@vintagemischief.com
Open Tues, Thurs- Sat 10-5pm

BECCLES
Market Place 1894
33335

The White Horse (far left), a pub since 1764, was run by William Beckett. The Peoples' Clothier (left) was Morris Sparling, then North's, and is now Coe's. On the right, both of the nearer buildings, one of which was Edward Masters, ironmongers, have been rebuilt. The last building is the Swan, a pub since 1538, run by John Fuller, who sold Morse's ales and stouts.

BECCLES
*From the Waveney
1894* 33333

The Waveney forms a natural boundary between Norfolk and Suffolk. Along the river frontage are boat yards, moorings and maltings. The church is unusual because the slope of the ground down to Puddingmore meant that the tower had to be built on firmer ground to the south-east of the building. Even so, it seems that the money ran out - the top storey was never added.

BUNGAY, *Market Place and the Black Dog of Bungay c1960* B617020

The dog was Black Shuck, who supposedly attacked worshippers at church here and at Blythburgh in 1557. The building, containing Davey's ('Baby Linen and Fancy Goods') and Reynolds grocer's shop, is virtually unchanged. To the right, along the curving line of the castle bailey, are S Ball & Sons and the Midland Bank, which has been rebuilt. The Pharmacy in the distance has lost its parapet and urns.

BUNGAY
The Butter Cross
c1955 B617014

The Butter Cross was built in 1689, after the fire of the previous year which destroyed much of the town. It has Tuscan columns and arches; the dome is crowned with a figure of Justice, added in 1754, with scales and sword but no blindfold. The stalls show that it is Market Day - Thursday. The building to the left of Cross Street is still a greengrocer's.

KESSINGLAND, *Beach Road c1965* K137008

On the left side of Ceylon House is the post office and to the right the grocer's and provision's shop, both run by William Lowrey. Today both businesses are in the right half of the building. The Victorian terraces and semi-detached houses are the same today. At the corner of Bethel Drive is the beach-flint Sailor's and Fisherman's Bethel (left), still functioning as a place of worship.

▶ **WRENTHAM**
High Street c1955
W444003

At the junction of the
A12 and B1177
(centre right) is an
advertisement for the
Spread Eagle Hotel,
kept by George Zessel,
whose father had the
White Hart at
Wickham Market.
Ahead are some
shops, including the
tea room and the
grocer and draper.
The two nearest
buildings on the left
were demolished
shortly after this date.
The outline can be
seen on the end of the
Basketwear building.

◀ **HOLTON**
The Village c1960
H383040

The post mill is dated
1752. It ceased working
in 1914, and later all the
machinery was removed.
Restoration was carried
out in 1966-68, and the
sails turned again for the
first time in 1998. The
central house was the
post office until 1997. The
further building is the
Lord Nelson, whose sign
has been moved to the
car park. Note the classic
bubble car of the period
(right).

▲ **HALESWORTH,** *The Thoroughfare c1955* H384028

Before the by-pass this was the main road through the town; it is now pedestrianised. On the left, Vanstone's, gents' outfitters, has a carved bressumer with figures that are linked to the Argentine family. J W Ebbs' electrical shop next door was once an ironmonger's, and was run by the father and grandfather of Sir David Frost. To the right, the shop with the Hovis sign is still a baker's; Jacksons has been rebuilt but remains an ironmonger's; and further on, the White Hart has become shops.

◄ **WANGFORD**
The Village 1895 36882

The post office, run by Robert Farrant, is on the left next to Strickland Cottage (is there a link with the author Agnes Strickland of Reydon?). In the gabled building was either Harry Benstead or William Terry, saddlers, followed by the Swan, run by Mrs Mary Newberry. At the very top of the street is the Lion, where George Hill was also a baker and confectioner.

▼ **WANGFORD,** *The Village 1895* 36883

The single-storey extension on the nearest house has been demolished, but there is something similar on the adjacent house. This was occupied by William Harvey, baker; the next, with the shop window covered, by William Baxter, butcher. The corner site was the former post office of 1879. At the bottom is the Angel, landlord John Copley, which is the only hostelry functioning today.

► **SOUTHWOLD**
North Cliff 1896 38621

The white building was the Coastguard Station, built in 1884-1904 here on the corner of South Parade to replace the Watch House, which was on the beach. Next to the flagpole is a signalling device. On the left, two boys in sailor suits talk to their mother; further on a boy with baskets delivers fish or bread; ladies promenade, and the carriages move slowly back and forth.

◄ **SOUTHWOLD**
Gunhill 1896
38626

The battery of six 18-pounders was presented to the town in 1745 by the Duke of Cumberland. Queen's Street is in the middle distance, and the lighthouse to the right. White Lodge with its balconies overlooks the sea (right). On the balcony of Gunhill Place two ladies are taking tea (left), while nearest to us, a lady with a parasol and a young boy sit as far apart as possible.

► **SOUTHWOLD**
The Lighthouse 1891 28354

The lighthouse, seen here from St James's Green, was built in 1890: 'the light is of 800 candle power and occulates twice every 20 seconds'. On the left are Adelaide Cottage and Caithness House. Several of the terraced houses have had bay windows added to the first floor rooms. The Sole Bay Inn was run by Mrs Maria Powditch. Beyond is the parish church, rebuilt 1430-60.

SOUTHWOLD
Market Place 1906
56845

All traffic has halted for the photographer, including the Great Eastern Railway bus (centre left). The Southwold narrow gauge railway, opened in 1879, linked the town to Halesworth and the main railway network. The large shop is Thomas Denny, grocer and draper. On the corner is Robert Critten, 'chymist'; further along the High Street are Stead & Simpson and the Crown Hotel.

FELIXSTOWE
AND SUFFOLK
COASTAL

WALBERSWICK, *The Ferry 1892* 29932

There has been a ferry between Southwold and Walberswick since at least the 13th century. The River Blyth Ferry Company was established in 1885 to provide a chain ferry to carry vehicles across the river. This was later replaced by a steam ferry which continued until 1942. This view shows the ferry at its mooring, awaiting custom. In the distance is the tower of Walberswick church, built in 1426.

WALBERSWICK
The Village 1892
29931

This was taken to the left of photograph 29932, but now from the Walberswick side of the river. We can see the house with a large chimney stack in both photographs. The tidal river is the remains of the Dunwich river, diverted in the storms of 1289. The annual British Open Crabbing Championships have been held here since 1980.

BLYTHBURGH, *The Church 1895* 36880

The church, situated on high ground above the river Blyth, is known locally as 'the Cathedral of the Marshes'. It was entirely rebuilt in the mid to late 15th century on a massive scale: it is 128 feet long with a tower 83 feet high, which had a spire until 1577. The large windows give a sense of light and awe to the interior.

◄ LEISTON
The Abbey 1922 72585

The abbey of the White Canons was transferred here from Minsmere in 1363, and rebuilt after a fire in 1382. In 1922 the site was owned by Miss Ellen Wrightson, who in 1946 bequeathed it to the Diocese. This view from the crossing shows the chancel, with the chapel of St Michael on the right and the chapel of St Mary, which had been restored in 1920, on the left.

◄ DUNWICH
The Priory Gateway 1910
62050

Following the ferocious storms of 1286-88, the River Blyth was diverted, the harbour partly blocked and huge areas of land were devoured by the sea, all of which marked the beginning of the decline of Dunwich. The Greyfriars had to move to this site for safety. Now the remains of the Priory are under threat once again from the sea.

▲ **THORPENESS,** *The Dunes Guesthouse 1929* 82983

Thorpeness was a planned seaside resort financed by Glencain Stuart Ogilvie in 1910-28 as a Tudor fantasy for the middle classes. On the right is The Dunes, built in 1914 as a guesthouse, and on the left is Barn Hall, later the Estate Office, built in 1925. Between the buildings is the Meare. Above the trees is the Water Tower, disguised as the House in the Clouds.

◄ THORPENESS
The Boat House 1922
72589

The 65-acre Meare was the first stage of the development. All the bays and islands are named in J M Barry style. The Boat House was built in 1911, before the Meare was completed. The houses on the left, built 1911-18, were to be the start of The Netherlands. The left one is Tulip Cottage and is decorated with tulips. The 'motor park' is behind the covered car.

ALDEBURGH
High Street 1909 62009

This photograph was taken from the entrance to the former East Suffolk Hotel, now the Aldeburgh Festival Office. Outside Constance and Ward's, the ironmongers (right), carts are parked at an angle, just as cars are today. On the left a baker makes deliveries, while two girls cycle to Arthur and James Fisher's shoe shop, now Butcher's. The buildings beyond the chemists have been radically altered or demolished.

► **ALDEBURGH**
The Moot Hall
1896 38669

The Moot Hall was built c1540 in the Market Place, but coastal erosion has left it on the seafront. The brickwork on the first floor dates from 1654, and so does the sundial with the inscription 'I only count the sunny hours'. To the right are the White Lion, which now incorporates the battlemented Gothic building next door, an 1870s terrace and the Wentworth Hotel.

◄ **YOXFORD**
The Village 1909
62052

This village is often called 'the Garden of Suffolk', something promoted by the local chemists Cleghorn and Owen, who produced the 'Garden of Suffolk Bouquet'. The turning on the right is to the Griffin, run by Henry Smith. Beside the church is the Three Tuns Hotel owned by David Beatton, which burnt down in January 1925. Lord Nelson and Charles Dickens are reputed to have stayed there.

▲ **YOXFORD,** *The Village Sign c1955* Y16003

Yoxford was among the first villages in Suffolk to have its own particular sign, which stands by the A12. The name means 'the ford which could be passed by a yoke of oxen' - thus the sign has an ox standing in water, framed by horns. The creation of signs such as these reflecting the history or origin of communities is widespread today.

◄ **KELSALE**
The Village c1955
K138002

This delightful group of contrasting buildings clusters along the river valley, with the church on higher ground to the north. The Eight Bells (left) closed in the 1980s and is now Peal House. Many other houses have a bell connection. The Post Office Stores on the corner closed in 1991. To the centre right is the Guildhall of c1495, with the Arts and Crafts-style Village Hall behind.

SAXMUNDHAM
The Village 1929 82949

The house on the left is The Firs, occupied by Miss Cooper. The garage (centre left) belongs to Smith and Wesby, agents for Morris with cars for hire, who are still there today. The building with Dutch gables beyond the crossroads is George Reynolds, butcher; then comes The Chocolate Box, Flora Clark, grocer, Leiston Co-op, and the Bell Hotel, owned by Frank Brown.

FRAMLINGHAM
Market Hill 1909 62028

This 16th-century building with an 18th-century façade was built after 1564 on the site of St Mary's Guildhall. Aubrey Thomas Wicks traded from London House. In an advertisement of 1907 he described his shop as 'the leading house in the District for Keen and Thrifty buyers of all kind of Millinery, Drapery, Ready made clothes, outfitting, Boots etc. All goods marked in plain figures at lowest City Prices'.

FRAMLINGHAM, *The Castle 1909* 62033

Framlingham, built 1190-1210, is amongst the earliest castles in England to be constructed with a fortified curtain wall. The Poor House (left) was built at the direction of Sir Robert Hitcham (d1636) who owned the castle. The gable wing dates from 1637, and the remainder from 1729. The Poor House, closed in the 1830s, had a variety of uses including, as here, a dwelling; in the 1980s it became a museum.

FRAMLINGHAM, *The Pump House 1929* 82072

A plaque inside explains that 'The funds for this water supply were promised by Ann Jeaffreson on September 29 1896, the day week preceding her sudden death. She gave the supply to Framlingham in tender Remembrance of her dear father and mother, William Jeaffreson (FRCS, 1844) and Cordelia his wife. Ho, everyone that thirsteth come you to the water: And he that hath no money come you'.

▼ **PARHAM,** *The Village 1929* 82084

The church tower still has a 14th-century bell frame, a rare survival. The thatched Old Parsonage at the end of the road is late 15th-century. The exposed timbers have been plastered over. A group of children stand by a 19th-century cottage now called White Gates. The double row of Street Cottages (right) is 17th-century; the further one is still three separate dwellings, and the nearer one was extended in the 1970s.

► **WICKHAM MARKET**
Market Hill 1929 82046

The man on the left is about to enter the shop of Cyril Amey, hairdresser and shopkeeper. There are then two 16th-century houses with jetties, but the grocer's shop is no longer on the corner. The building on the other side is still a butcher's, but the White Hart Hotel run by Louis Zissell has closed.

◄ **WICKHAM MARKET**
Market Hill 1929
82048

We start with the White Hart (left); then comes A J White, watch and clockmaker (the other half of the building was Barclay's Bank, open on Wednesdays), George Howe, draper and grocer, Adam's, baker and confectioner, and the Crown, run by George Harris. In the corner is The Grange, a Georgian-fronted building with a fine doorway. The church tower is octagonal and capped with a wooden leaded spire. The pump has been replaced with a car park.

► **WICKHAM MARKET**
Bridge Street 1929
82049

This road, also called Lower Street, leads towards the mill. On the left is the late 17th-century Chequers, where Mrs Edith Turtel offered 'Garage Accommodation for Motors and Cyclists'. The pub closed in 1999. Opposite is the Ipswich Industrial Co-operative Society, with separate butchery and grocery departments. Further on was T T Mullins & Co, basket and sieve manufacturers.

WICKHAM MARKET
The Mill 1929 82056

The mill complex was owned by Reuben Rackham, who was a maltster, water and steam miller and a coal merchant. The watermill is late 18th-century, with a cast iron breast-shot wheel and three pairs of stones. The early 19th-century Mill House has a two-storey central window. The bridge over the tailrace, partly built in hachestone, has rails and posts inscribed 'A Barnes Woodbridge 1901'.

PETTISTREE, *The Church 1929* 82060

The 15th-century tower has flushwork patterns on the battlements and buttresses. Below the nave roof is a row of blocked windows, indicating that there was a plan to build an aisle, which was never carried out. The Greyhound was probably the medieval Guildhall. The landlord in 1929 was William Brooks. The building is unchanged except for the addition of a porch.

BUTLEY
The Street and the Post Office c1955
B618003

The shop had been run by Robert Hazelwood since the 1880s. His son Robert and his grandchildren continued at the shop and post office until its closure in September 1975. The wooden buildings were replaced by a house in the 1980s. Through the telegraph pole we can see the roof of the former forge, owned for many years by the Burch family.

BUTLEY, *The Priory c1955* B618010

This priory of Augustinian canons was founded in 1171. The gatehouse of 1320-25 is the only structure that remains. The other side has magnificent flatwork decoration and rows of heraldry. This side of the gateway has a row of flushwork arches above the entrance, and over it is a window flanked by 'windows' in flushwork. In the gable is a flushwork 10-spoked wheel.

ORFORD
The Church, Norman Arches 1909 62021

Several coastal churches, including the one at Orford, have been reduced in size by blocking off the eastern end. These parishes were wealthy ports in the medieval period when the churches were built, but then suffered decline when their harbours silted up or trade decreased. At Orford the chancel of c1166 was an outstanding piece of Norman architecture six bays long with vaulted aisles, of which only these arches remain.

ORFORD, *The Castle 1937* 88243

The keep was built in 1165-73 by Henry II as a check on the power of Hugh Bigod, Earl of Norfolk and Suffolk, who had castles at Framlingham and Bungay. Orford had a revolutionary new design of a towered keep with curving walls, which withstood the rebellion of 1173. All the other buildings of the castle complex have been destroyed over time.

ORFORD
Market Hill 1937
88241

There had been a Monday market here since 1154, but it ceased in the Victorian period. The Manor House (centre left) with its 19th-century brick façade is central to the market place. The houses to the left have been replaced, and those beyond restored. The church lost the top of its tower in 1829, and it was not repaired until the 1960s. The area is never as car-free today.

BAWDSEY, *The Manor 1899* 43241

The house was built in 1866-1905 by Sir Cuthbert Quilter, MP and stockbroker. Here we see the construction still under way. It is said that Quilter added a new tower for each million he made - by 1905 there were nine towers. In 1936 the Air Ministry purchased Bawdsey Manor, and here Sir Robert Watson Watts led the team that developed radar - so crucial in the Battle of Britain.

◄ **MELTON**
Wilford Bridge 1898
42775

Wilford, meaning 'willow ford', was the meeting place for the Anglo-Saxon administrative area later called Wilford Hundred. The bridge carries the road over the River Deben, where a short-lived quay was built in the 19th century. A bridge of 1764 was replaced by this one of white brick and stone in 1798. The floods of 1939 resulted in a new single span bridge being erected.

◄ **MELTON**
High Street
c1955 M268007

Three of the four terrace houses on the right were once shops. On the opposite corner, Skoulding's grocer's and draper's had traded since the 1850s. Here the premises are a café and shop; they are now a restaurant, although most of the shop front has been retained. The houses in the distance, beyond the lady with the pram, have been demolished and replaced by Thurlow's.

▲ **WOODBRIDGE,** *Church Street 1906* 53500

Opposite is the shop of George Booth, bookseller and stationer, who produced the Woodbridge Almanac. The overhanging jetty is supported by two cast iron Doric columns. The cornice with its modest claim has now been removed. Further on is the 18th-century red brick Arnott House. Between them the first-floor windows are about to be cleaned. St Mary's rectory is on the right.

◄ **WOODBRIDGE**
The Promenade 1906
53495

This shows the raised riverbank as a place of recreation, with seats, shelters and a bandstand. A barge makes towards the dock, passing the coal jetty on the left. On the skyline are several maltings, shipyards, Buss's Dock and the tide mill. The bandstand has been rebuilt with a brick base, and all the shelters are now of brick.

WOODBRIDGE
The Promenade 1925
78746

When this similar view was taken 27 years after No 53495, the Promenade had taken on a more seafront appearance. The paved terrace has since gone as part of the more recent flood prevention scheme. Beyond the bandstand are Alfred Everson, boat builder at the Phoenix works, and the Deben Rowing Club. Ahead are the Station House, the theatre, shipyards, and cranes on the dock.

▼ **WOODBRIDGE,** *The Quayside 1925* 78747

There has been a tide mill here since at least the 12th century, although the present building dates from c1793. The mill operated for about two hours each low tide as the water, trapped in the mill pond on the high tide, was released. The mill ceased to work in 1957; it was restored in the 1970s, and is now the last working tide mill on the east coast.

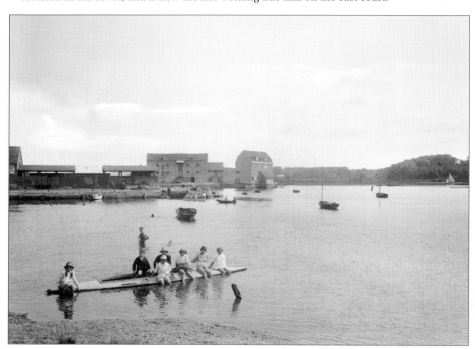

▶ **WOODBRIDGE**
The Beach 1898 42773

This was taken from Buss's Dock looking down river. Children are playing at the water's edge and on Ferry Dock; boats rest in the channel; a yacht is being painted; and people relax in the ornate shelter. The Woodbridge Regatta was held here intermittently since 1838. The Deben Sailing Club and the Woodbridge Rowing Club from 1906 made it an annual event.

◄ WALDRINGFIELD
The Sailing Club House and the Beach c1960
W438045

In the second half of the 19th century there was a large trade here in coprolite and cement. George Mason ran a cement works here from c1870 to 1907, when the process transferred to Claydon. In 1921 the Sailing Club was founded, and the Club House was built in 1932. It was extended several times and rebuilt in 1981. The steps lead up to the Maybush.

► TRIMLEY
The Village and the Church 1899
43248

The two churches of St Martin and St Mary stand adjacent to each other in the same churchyard. St Mary's tower was a ruin at this time; it was not until 1960 that it was restored in memory of Mrs Josselyn. On the left is the site of the Welcome Hall of 1902 and of the Three Mariners, kept by Mrs Elizabeth Elliott.

FELIXSTOWE
Constable Road 1907
58976

This area was developed after 1885 on land owned by the Freehold Land Society. In the distance is the newly-opened Felix Hotel of 1903. On the corner of Gainsborough Road Mr Chapman stands outside his shop (right), with an advertisement for Frederick Tibbenham, a cabinetmaker at No 19, beyond him. On the left the baker is delivering to No 46, one of the many decorative terraced houses in the road.

FELIXSTOWE
The Mansion 1899
43239

This Italianate mansion was built c1860 for Mr Eley, the cartridge manufacturer, and was known locally as 'Eley Cathedral'. It was here that the German Empress stayed in 1891. Her three-week stay gave impetus to the popularity of Felixstowe, which became 'the Queen of East Coast Resorts'. Coincidentally, waters equal to those of Spa in Germany were also discovered in 1891.

FELIXSTOWE, *High Beach 1907* 58959

The pair of wooden houses were called Montpelier in 1885; the next building is of 1889, and the building partly hidden by trees was Harland House in 1885. The gabled building on the right is part of the stable block dated 1904 which belonged to the adjacent Fludyer Arms of 1902. The stay of Mrs Simpson, the future wife of the Duke of Windsor, at Beach House is commemorated in the modern tea room in the old stables.

FELIXSTOWE
Sea Road 1907 58970

In the distance is Martello Tower Q, built in 1808-10 as a defence against French invasion. The nearest building was the Anchorage, which had been extended in 1891 by adding the section with balconies and the unusually-angled gable end. In 1907 it was extended again and became St Mary's Children's Home. In the street the carriages ply their trade, while the postman delivers letters.

FELIXSTOWE, *The Ferry Boat Inn 1907* 58990

Sir Cuthbert Quilter established a steam-drawn chain ferry between Felixstowe and Bawdsey. The two ferry boats, commissioned in 1894, were the 'Lady Quilter' and the 'Lady Beatrice'; they operated until 1931. In the foreground children make daisy chains and play with a cart, while a delivery is made to Margaret Rogers, landlady of the Ferry Boat Inn.

IPSWICH
TOWN AND DOCKS

IPSWICH, *The Docks 1921* 70412

This view looks across the Entrance Lock towards Cliff Brewery, behind the trees, with Cliff Quay to the right. The eight spritsail barges wait to bring their cargoes into the dock. Spritsails were the last working barges in northern Europe, continuing until the early 1960s. The main cargoes brought into Ipswich were grain, barley, coal and timber.

▼ **IPSWICH,** *The Ancient House 1899* 44505

This is the most spectacular house in Ipswich, redesigned c1670 by the Sparrow family. The first floor has oriel windows, in the centre of which are the arms of Charles II. The plasterwork under each window represents Europe, Asia, Africa and America, the latter with a tobacco pipe. In 1899 the house was occupied by Frederick Pawsey, printer and bookseller.

▶ **IPSWICH**
Westgate Street 1893
32200

We are looking east towards the Presbyterian church of 1870. On the right is the Crown and Anchor Hotel, whose landlord was Charles Quilter. Then came James Juby, tailor, and Garrards, wine merchants. On the corner was the Provincial Co-operative Drug Co (centre), and next was the Barley Mow tavern run by William Ellis. On the left are Frederick Raphael ('German Fancy Goods'), Frederick Betts, confectioner, and John Holland, hairdresser.

◄ IPSWICH
*The Corn
Exchange 1893*
32203

The earlier Corn
Exchange on Cornhill
was demolished in
1880 for the new post
office. The
replacement was built
in 1882 in a mixture of
Italianate styles, with
French pavilions on
the roof. This front
towards King Street
had shops on the
ground floor, one of
which was the Essex
and Suffolk Fire Office.
The building became
a film theatre in 1973.

► IPSWICH
*Christchurch Park
House 1893* 32217

Christchurch was built
by Edmund Withypoll in
1548-50, of red brick, on
the site of Holy Trinity
Priory. In 1893 the house
and park were offered
for sale. The house was
purchased and given to
the town in 1895 by Felix
Cobbold, on condition
that the Corporation
bought the park. The
house became a
museum, and the park
and the arboretum a
pleasure ground.

STOWMARKET AND MID SUFFOLK

CLAYDON, *Main Road c1955* C510006

This is the junction of Station Road (right) and, until the by-pass was opened, the main Stowmarket to Ipswich road. In the foreground is the Greyhound, with a delivery being made to the side door. On the left are two buildings, now one, with the village stores which were refurbished in 1990. The bus has stopped outside the Crown to pick up passengers.

▲ **DEBENHAM**
High Street 1950 D121013

On the right are Rayner's, an electrical shop, and Thomas the ironmonger. To the right, the long building is the former 15th-century Guildhall. At this end was Mick Ellis the tailor, and at the other was Barclay's Bank. The 15th-century Red Lion, beyond, closed in 2000. Next door was Watson's the chemists. The brick building (centre) was Carter's cycle shop, and beyond it was Wells' the electrician.

◄ **EYE**
The Town Hall c1960 E245006

The Town Hall is in the middle of the ancient market place. It was designed in 1857 by Edward Lamb of Manchester, using an unusual combination of bricks and flints in the main building, the tower and the cupola. Eye, the second oldest borough in Suffolk (1408) and the smallest borough in the United Kingdom, lost its status in 1974.

► **EYE**
Church Street c1960
E245009

Behind the thatched cottage in Church Street, where the author's great-uncle and great-aunt lived in the late 19th century, is the castle mound built in 1066-71 by William Mallet. The ruin on top is a folly erected in 1844 by General Sir Edward Kerrison. The church stands outside the castle bailey. The tower is 101 feet high, and was built c1454-79.

◄ **LAXFIELD**
Low Road c1955
L361009

The 17th-century thatched King's Head is amongst the best-known pubs in Suffolk. The Felgate family were licensees from c1880 until 1970. Its attraction is that it remains an old-fashioned pub with no frills. Beer is drawn from barrels in the taproom, while customers are entertained by traditional musicians and singers. The 'Low House' was East Anglian Pub of the Year in 2000.

▲ **METFIELD,** *Main Street c1955* M269007

This is taken from outside the Duke William. The roofline and dormer windows of the cottage on the left have subsequently been altered. The building at right angles to the road (centre) is the medieval Guildhall. Rose Cottage, nearest to us, with classical heads on either side of the door, was rebuilt in 1904 by William Taylor, a member of the manorial family.

◄ **NEEDHAM MARKET**
St John's Church 1922
71936

Needham, on the main road, was in ancient times a hamlet of Barking, but only became a parish in 1901. Although it looks like a Victorian chapel, the church has the most splendid hammer-beam roof in the country. Beyond is Pillar House, a timber-framed building with a Victorian brick façade. On the next corner is the 16th-century Bull (John Esling was the landlord), now closed.

NEEDHAM MARKET
Hawkes Mill c1960
N155028

The central section of the brick watermill was built in 1884, and the wings were added in 1892. The road is carried over the millrace by an 18th-century bridge. The River Gipping, made navigable in 1793, is off to the right, with locks which enable barges to go upstream. The mill has since been converted into dwellings.

BARKING TYE
The Village 1934
86418

This looks like Sunday morning, with people either returning from the church or heading towards the chapel on the Tye. Walnut Tree is on the right, with Wayside and Apple Tree Cottage on the left. Land here was owned by the Quaker Philip Butler, Secretary of the Suffolk Tithe Payers' Association, which helped to bring about the abolition of tithes in 1936.

BARKING TYE, *Brown's Farm 1934* 86419

The thatched Brown's farm, on Willisham Road, was one of several in the area owned by Jack Gibbons. The unidentified youth with the trilby hat is probably bringing the flock back to the confines of the farmyard for shearing.

STOWMARKET
The River 1922 71948

We are looking west from the canal towpath towards the town, with the church spire in the centre distance. The industrial complex is the tannery of Edward Stow, established in Milton Road from 1896 to 1904. There are maltings against the skyline to the right. Out of view to the right are the railway line and the Suffolk Iron Foundry.

STOWMARKET, *The Cattle Market c1955* S583004

The cattle market was off Crow Street, adjacent to the ancient market place. Between the 1930s and 1970s this was one of the largest pig markets in the county. In addition to weekly livestock markets, there were spring and autumn sales for store cattle. The sale yard was run by R C Knights until its closure in the mid 1980s. It is now partly Asda Supermarket.

STOWMARKET
Tavern Street c1955
S583002

We are looking west towards Station Road and the church - the delicate spire was added to the tower in 1712. The British Legion (left) remains today, but the Stowmarket Co-op next door has been rebuilt. On the corner is Fidler's, menswear, taken over by Tydeman's in 1997. On the right is Stannard's, now in rebuilt premises, but here since c1916 and inventors of the Stannard Safety Cycle.

▼ **WOOLPIT,** *The Swan Inn c1960* W442019

The inn occupied both of these buildings. The one to the left is 16th-century, with a brick façade of 1759. The taller building was erected in 1826. The inn has closed, the urn has gone from the niche, and the petrol pumps have been removed. The village pump commemorates Queen Victoria's Jubilee in 1897. The corners of the shelter are carved with the queens Boadicea, Elizabeth, Anne and Victoria.

▶ **WOOLPIT**
Main Street c1955
W442007

Most of the buildings are timber-framed, although it is only at the far end that they retain their original appearance. This group includes the Bull (centre left) and the late 15th-century Weaver's House beyond the parked car. On the right is a former 16th-century pub with a decorative Victorian front. The shop at the near corner is Addison's, established in 1889.

◄ **WOOLPIT**
The Market Place c1960 W442026

This view is taken from the top of the church tower overlooking the triangular market place, with the Jubilee Pump and Swan Inn. The building to the left is the 16th-century Village Institute, now also a thriving museum, which was restored and enlarged in 1920 as the Village War Memorial. The high elevation enables us to see the typically flat agricultural land of West Suffolk.

▶ **BEYTON**
The White Horse Inn c1955 B877004

The White Horse is a timber-framed building of 1694, later encased in Victorian brick when the far bay was added. On the left is the corner of the shop, with its penny bubble gum dispenser. The former agency for the County Fire Office is Rous's cycle shop (right). This was demolished to widen the road shortly after the photo was taken.

SUDBURY AND BABERGH

PIN MILL
The River Orwell 1909 61999

Before the deepening of the channel to Ipswich, ships stopped at Butterman's Bay to be unloaded into barges from Pin Mill. Arthur Ransome described Pin Mill with its 'crowd of yachts and its big brown sailed barges and steamers going up to Ipswich or down to the sea'. Esther Garrard, one of three boat builders, has her yard over on the left.

WOOLVERSTONE
Woolverstone Hall c1960 W443001

Woolverstone Hall was built in 1776 by William Berners overlooking the Orwell, up-river from Pin Mill. This is the entrance front; the rows of Nissen huts and a water tank above the roofline are features of the former Nautical School, linked to HMS 'Ganges'. The Hall became an LCC boarding grammar school in 1950, and more recently Ipswich High School for Girls.

EAST BERGHOLT, *Burnt Oak c1955* E247037

The area of Burnt Oak was centred on the King's Head, just off to the right. The shop offers an alternative to alcohol by offering teas and snacks, in a time before pub food was the norm. The long building on the right was the parish Town House, or Poor House, purchased in 1654 and in use until 1834.

EAST BERGHOLT
St Mary's Church
c1955 E247025

The church was rebuilt in the late 15th century. The western tower was started later in 1525 with a stone base and, as at nearby Dedham, a vaulted ground floor with processional arches in the north and south sides. But through lack of funds the tower was never finished. John Constable made several sketches and paintings of this, his native parish church.

EAST BERGHOLT, *The Bell Cage c1960* E247070

The bell cage was erected in the early 16th century, probably as a temporary measure while the tower was rebuilt. The cage is not unique, but the method of ringing is. The bells are swung by the ringer standing on the bell-frame, pushing the bells over. Ringing ceased following an accident in 1999, but following alterations the bells were rung again on New Year's Day in 2002.

FLATFORD
Bridge House c1960
F31051

Bridge House and the bridge over the Stour are now owned by the National Trust. To the right of the photograph is a dry dock where lighters were repaired - it is shown in Constable's painting 'Boatbuilding' (1814). The dock was recently restored by the National Trust and the Stow River Trust.

◀ **HADLEIGH**
The Guildhall 1922
71975

The central section was the Market House, and dates from c1450. The wing to the left was added as the Guildhall. It was later partly under-built in brick, hence the loss of the jetty. The ground floor was used as almshouses. The right-hand extension is 18th-century, and was part of the Grammar School. A town hall was built adjacent to the complex in 1851.

◀ **FLATFORD**
The Mill 1907
57551

This shows the overflow pond which was the location of Constable's 'The Haywain' (1821). The mill, which dates from c1730, occupies the site of a mill which has stood here since at least the 14th century. The mill house was the home of Golding Constable and his family from 1765 to 74, and it remained in their possession until the 1840s. Flour was taken downstream by lighters to Mistley for London.

▲ **HADLEIGH,** *Dr Taylor's Memorial 1922* 71985

This marks the spot on Aldham Common where Rowland Taylor, Rector of Hadleigh, was burnt in 1555. His curate Richard Yeoman was burnt at Norwich in 1558. This monument to them both was erected by public subscription in 1818, to replace an earlier one which was placed within the rails. 'This is the Victory that overcometh the World, even our Faith'.

◀ **HADLEIGH**
Row Chapel 1922 71984

Under the will of Archdeacon Pykenham, twelve almshouses were built in 1490 on either side of the earlier wayside chapel of St. Mary Magdalene and Catherine of Sienna. The present chapel is late 15th-century and timber-framed. It was restored in 1891 by Charles Spooner, an architect of the Arts and Crafts movement, which is reflected in its furnishings and fittings.

KERSEY
The Village c1955
K136027

This view, looking from the church tower towards the water-splash of the Brett, shows a very different regard for timber-framed buildings from today. The thatched cottage on the right has an early AA metal sign, giving mileages to local villages. The next building down had been Goymour's the butchers until 1950. Beyond the splash is the timbered Bell Inn, and above it is Stay Barn.

▼ **KERSEY,** *The Splash c1955* K136031

The building on the left was Mr Lemon the vet's, and has a horse's tail hanging at the far end. To the right with the bay window is the sweet shop run by the King family until the 1980s. It was at the splash that the fictional antique dealer Lovejoy first met Lady Jane Felsham by drenching her and frightening the Muscovy ducks!

► **CHELSWORTH**
The Bridge and the Peacock Inn c1960
C746012

This is taken from the 'tongues' in the middle of the River Brett, adjacent to the two 18th-century hump-backed bridges. The Peacock is early 15th-century. The shop, which closed in 1977, was in the gable wing. The beerhouse and shop were run together; the former was called the Peacock after the mother of the two sisters who sold it to the brewery.

◄**MONKS ELEIGH**
The Village c1955
M270024

In this view the church seems to close the end of the village green. The three groups of cottages are timber-framed and date from the 17th and 18th centuries. There is a white brick Gothic battlemented arch between the first and second group. The pump was the gift of William Makin, farmer at the Hall, in 1854; it was made by Ransomes & Sims of Ipswich.

► **BILDESTON**
Duke Street c1955
B766020

Just off to the left is the site of the earliest Baptist chapel in Suffolk, registered in 1731. Towards the end is the Brotherhood Hall, later Duke's Hall, built in the early 1920s by unemployed ex-servicemen. At the end is Red House, a Tudor farmhouse with a brick front of c1715. The school playground is on the right.

HITCHAM
The Village c1960
H382001

This shows Old Hall (the former medieval Guildhall), the church, Church Lane, Friday Cottage (far right), Fen Lane with its finger post, and the bridge over the river Brett. One of the cottages in the row was occupied by Frederick Butcher, the parish gravedigger. The three were converted into one in the late 1990s, although the positions of the doors and windows can still be seen under the plasterwork.

LAVENHAM, *Market Place c1955* L21006

The market cross dates from 1500, and was intended to be a copy of the one at Cambridge. To the right is the former Market Toll House, adjoining the British School of 1861. The Great House (left) was the home of the poet Stephen Spender in the late 1930s. The timbered Little Hall next door of 1425-50 is now the home of the Suffolk Preservation Society.

LAVENHAM
The Church 1895 35497

This is one of the best-known churches in Suffolk. Apart from the chancel, the entire church was rebuilt in c1485-1525. The finance was provided by the de Veres, the Springs and other families, most of whom were connected with the cloth trade. Cliff Richard performed here at a Mission in 1972, and the author and his wife Dorothy were married here in 1973.

BOXFORD, *Church Street c1955* B620021

The building in the foreground was the Chequers, an alehouse since the early 15th century, which closed in 1939. The room over the archway was the Reading Room, later a school room for evacuees during the war. The house beyond is the Forge, run by the Stone family, who were also parish sextons. Walter Bowers is driving the carrier's cart.

▼ **ASSINGTON,** *The Village 1907* 58915

The post office (note the recruiting posters on its wall, right) was kept by Henry Chatters.
Beyond is the Shoulder of Mutton, whose landlord Frederick Godday was also a butcher.
The white gabled building (centre left) has been the post office since the 1940s. At the end is
the School House, occupied by Richard Cobb. The school was built in 1844 and closed in 1984.

▶ **BURES**
Suffolk Knoll c1955
B324006

Maynscroft restaurant and
café and the adjoining
William's cycle shop (right)
closed shortly after 1955
and became dwellings. The
Queen's Head closed in
c1990 and is now a
restaurant. The empty
building has been
demolished, while
Chambers still run their
coaches from the tall gabled
building. Opposite on the
corner of Bridge Street is
the shop run by Len Mylott
in the 1950s.

◄ **SUDBURY**
Market Hill and the Church 1907 58907

Amongst the shops on the left are the Bazaar of the Misses Parsonson, Robert Joy's carpet warehouse, John Payn, stationer and printer, William Brampton, chemist, and James Read, furniture dealer (both these latter are now Boot's). The familiar statue of Thomas Gainsborough in front of St Peter's was not erected until 1913. Note the double step from the pavement to the left.

► **GREAT CORNARD**
The Church 1900 45083

The church had been restored in 1862 and the south aisle, with square headed windows, had been rebuilt in 1887. Apart from the loss of the gable cross and the insertion of clock dials into the tower, the view is unchanged today. The white gravestone is in memory of Edward Baker, owner of Cornard Mills (d1891) and Elisabeth his wife (d1917).

SUDBURY, *Market Hill 1900* 45068

The red brick building is Lloyd's Bank, dated 1879. Next is Robert Joy, draper and milliner (he also had the shop opposite), and then Bruno, baker and confectioner, with the large window on the first floor. The first two shops in the next building were owned by Arthur Brook, glass and china dealer. Agricultural implements are laid out for sale - it is Saturday, market day.

SUDBURY
The Market 1904
51156A

Sudbury had a corn and cattle market on Thursdays with a general market on Saturdays. There was also an annual pony sale, attended by travellers, on Market Hill. Despite the stalls, agricultural implements, horses and ponies, the attraction is the Punch and Judy show outside St Peter's, which is enthralling young, old and even the carriage trade.

SUDBURY, *Friars Street 1895* 35468

The street takes its name from the priory of Dominican friars, founded in the 13th century. The tree marks the site of the now demolished Congregational church. Beyond the draper's awning is the Quaker Meeting House and Buzzards, the home of Thomas Gainsborough's uncle Thomas. Two of the artist's daughters were born in the fourth house on the right in 1750 and 1751.

SUDBURY
Floodgate Pool 1932
85147

This is part of the Sudbury
Common Lands. The sluice
gate is to the left, and the
cattle stand in the overflow,
or floodpool. On the
horizon are the towers of
the Catholic church and
St Gregory's. The mill lode is
marked by willow trees, and
behind them to the right is
Walnut Tree Hospital, the
former workhouse.

► **LONG MELFORD**
The Green 1906
55557

In the distance is the late 15th-century church, partly obscured by the Holy Trinity Hospital founded in 1573 by Sir William Cordell. At the road junction is the Black Lion, rebuilt in 1839, and a grocer's known as Top Shop. The Tudor houses have been subdivided to provide houses for the poorer members of the village. The children have just come out of the National School.

◄ **LONG MELFORD**
The Bull Hotel c1955
L101002

The building dates from c1450 and has been an inn since at least 1580. It had been covered by a brick façade, which was removed in 1935. The posts on either side of the doorway have initials for the Drew family and the date 1649. Two cottages to the right were rebuilt in the 1960s and incorporated into the hotel, retaining the chimneystack.

▲ **LONG MELFORD,** *Kentwell Hall 1895* 35495

This moated E-shaped house was started by William Clopton in c1540 and extended in the 1560s and 1590s. The Cloptons had co-ordinated the rebuilding of the church in the late 15th century. The mile-long avenue of lime trees leading to the house was planted in 1678. In 1895 the house was owned by Edward Starkie Bence, but let to Henry Norton.

◄ **HARTEST**
The Stone c1955
H380009

In the distance the church and the Crown are hidden by trees. To the left is the Congregational chapel, opened in 1864, with round-headed windows added in 1906. The chapel closed in 1980. The gable end is part of a 15th-century Wealden house. The stone was brought here from Somerton in 1713 on a sledge pulled by 45 horses to commemorate the Treaty of Utrecht.

BURY AND ST EDMUNDSBURY

HAVERHILL
Market Place c1950 H381004

As a result of the expansion of the town since 1959 due to London overspill, much of the center was redeveloped. The buildings in the distance, including National Stores and Jarvis, the butchers, have been demolished. The grand building was the Corn Exchange of 1889. On the right are Barclay's Bank, Merchant's, haberdashers, the post office, Bell, the Co-op (with dome), and Poole's, furnishers.

▼ **CLARE,** *Market Hill c1960* C512002

On the left is a terrace of brick houses and shops built c1865. Barclay's Bank closed in 2000, but the Co-op still trades from the ground floor, although it now has a mid-1990s shop front. Wilkins's garage closed c1985; next door was Bruce's, watchmaker, with the butchers on the corner. On the right is the Town Hall of 1912-13.

▶ **CAVENDISH**
The Church c1960
C509011

These cottages on the green, against the backdrop of the church, are probably the most photographed houses in Suffolk. Church Cottages, or Hyde Park Corner Cottages, are five almshouses run by the George Savage Trust. In 1971 they were severely damaged by fire, and were rebuilt and reopened in 1972. To the left is the sign of the Five Bells.

BURY ST EDMUNDS
The Abbey Gate
1898 41229

This was the main entrance to the secular part of the Abbey of St Edmunds. The original gate was probably a duplicate of the Norman tower. It was destroyed during the riot of 1327 and rebuilt in the Decorated style. The earlier gate stood further to the left, and the join in the wall shows its position. The portcullis is a Victorian replacement.

BURY ST EDMUNDS
The Corn Exchange
1922 71954

This was built in 1861-62. The portico has a central medallion with Queen Victoria's head, flanked by figures representing bounty and agriculture. In 1969-70 a floor was inserted and shops were created on the ground floor. To the left is Everards Hotel, owned by William Emms. The drinking fountain of 1870, which was moved to the Abbey Gardens in 1939, was given by the Marquis of Bristol.

BURY ST EDMUNDS
Cornhill c1955 B258044

The large building is the
Market Cross and Theatre,
built by the Adam brothers in
1774-80. To the left the shops
include Hepworth's, Home and
Colonial, and International
Stores. On the right are
L D Faires, wine merchants;
Annette's, ladies' fashions; and,
under the lock sign, Henshall's,
ironmongers. Beyond is the
1930s Woolworth's, which took
over from Henshall's in 1959.

▶ PAKENHAM
The Windmill c1965 P286063

The brick tower mill was built in c1820 to replace an earlier mill. It was damaged by storms in 1948 and repaired in 1950, when a gallery was added to the cap. The Bryant family have owned and maintained the mill since 1920. The turning windmill was used as one of the Intermissions between BBC television programmes in the 1950s.

▼ GREAT BARTON
The Round House c1960 G338004

This was the thatched lodge gate from the village street to the Hall. It dates from the 1840s, when Sir Henry Bunbury created the park around the Hall. The gate was to the left, and survives today at the entrance to St John's. The Hall burnt down in 1914, and the estate was sold in 1915. The drive now gives access to areas of housing.

▶ IXWORTH
The Old Mill c1955 I76011

The watermill was disused in 1955, but it was subsequently restored. The structure is timber-framed with a weatherboard exterior. The cast-iron breast shot waterwheel is inside the building and is dated 1800, with the initials of John Lowe, the miller. The mill house to the right is early 17th-century with later additions and alterations.

◄ **IXWORTH**
*The Lime Tree,
High Street c1955*
I76034

The lime tree, shown on the 1846 Tithe map, was uprooted in an accident in December 1971. However, it was included in the village sign in 1973, and a new tree is growing nearby. The house and shop to the left have been demolished. Off to the left are the first rural council houses in England, built in 1893.

NEWMARKET AND FOREST HEATH

NEWMARKET, *The Clock Tower 1922* 71916

The red brick clock tower was erected in 1890 to commemorate Queen Victoria's Jubilee of 1887. There were drinking fountains on three sides, with an inscription reading '1837 Jubilate Victoriae 1887'. To the right is Thompson's Dining Room, later the Jubilee Tea Rooms, but now rebuilt. Further right is Aberdeen House, now occupied by Judith Fisher.

NEWMARKET
The War Memorial 1929 81960

In Bury Road is the Memorial Garden, formerly part of the Severalls. The grey granite war memorial has the names of the fallen on the base, an inscription on the column and is surmounted by an everlasting flame. The names of the 27 people who were killed in the 1941 bombing raid are about to be added to the memorial.

NEWMARKET, *The Jockey Club Rooms 1922* 71922

This strange mixture of classical styles formed the façade of the Jockey Club until 1935. Following a fire, the present building was designed in 1938 by Sir Albert Richardson. It incorporated the original coffee house which the club purchased in 1770 when they moved here from London. The National Horseracing Museum is behind the left section of the façade.

NEWMARKET
High Street 1922 71915

On the left is Gilbert and Sons, saddler and harness maker. Ahead, with a classical Georgian front, is the Rutland Arms of 1815. The mock timber-framed Chestnuts now has a shop front at ground level. The butcher's beyond has been rebuilt as a bank. Beyond it is the 16th-century Wagon and Horses -the livestock market was held in its yard.

► **NEWMARKET**
High Street 1929
81958

Unsaddled horses are being led down the street. Could they be going to a Tattersalls sale? A man, a window cleaner and two children watch the horses from beneath the awning of Jessie Blyth, milliner; next door is William Parker, jeweller and optician. Further on, a restaurant serves luncheons and teas to those walking to the races.

◄ **NEWMARKET**
High Street 1929
81956

On the left is the King Edward VII Memorial Hall of 1914, with pleasure gardens behind. The building with two gables is the White Hart, damaged in the air raid of 18 February 1941. To the right is the Comet Kinema, which became the Kingsway from 1926 until 1977. Further on are the Jockey Club and a large shop, now Palmer's, dated 1832.

▲ **EXNING,** *Chapel Street c1955* E246002

The post office on the corner has advertisements for the Doric Cinema, Newmarket. The post office and its sign have now been transferred to the second terrace house. Further down the street is the gable of the Methodist chapel. In the distance is the sign of the Wheatsheaf. The building on the left is dated 1883, and the two shops have now become offices.

◄ **BARTON MILLS**
The Village 1925 78285

Until the by-pass was opened, this was the route of the A11. This group of buildings (dated 1668) flanks the bridge over the River Lark, which provided power for the water mill. John Godfrey installed a steam engine and roller milling plant in the 1880s. Parker Brothers took over the mill in c1900 and sold it in 1948, after which it was demolished.

MILDENHALL
Market Place 1925
78277

In the centre are the pump, in use until 1939, and the 16th-century Market Cross. On the right are Mabel Kemp's cycle shop and Isaac Minn's, saddler. In the High Street, the house (centre left) will soon be the shop of Henry Stile's gent's outfitters; in the centre are the Tiger's Head, landlord Edward Smith, and the gabled Boot Stores of 1905.

MILDENHALL, *High Street c1955* M75009

The Bell (right) has been an inn since the 1790s. Next door, Busson and Parkin, ironmongers, traded here from 1928 to 1968. The White Hart (centre) was rebuilt after a fire in 1910. The plastered building was Judkin's, which is now part of the pub. The corner building had the plaster removed in 1932, when it became Barclay's Bank. The Market Cross can just be seen in the distance.

MILDENHALL
Mill Street 1925 78280

On the left are Harry Webber, hairdresser, in the former Oakes Bank of 1885, the International Stores (Frederick Riches was manager), who traded here from 1909 to 1976, and Eccleston's, draper and grocers, now the post office. To the right with the awning are Charles Brown, tailor, with a shop front of 1888, Charles Stebbing, shoemaker, and Simpson's Printing Works, where the Mildenhall Almanac and Directory was published from 1873 to 1946.

BRANDON, *The River Ouse 1925* 78268

Parts of this bridge may date from the 1670s, when the river was made navigable. The Borough of Thetford had the right of tolls until 1872 and was responsible for its repair until 1950. There was an extensive river trade in malt, corn, coal, gunflints and rabbit skins. The bridge was replaced in 1954. The Ouse River Hotel (centre right) was run by Arthur Rolph.

THORPENESS, *The Benthills 1929* 82979

INDEX

Frith Book Co Titles

www.francisfrith.co.uk

The Frith Book Company publishes over 100 new titles each year. A selection of those currently available are listed below. For latest catalogue please contact Frith Book Co.
Town Books 96 pages, approximately 100 photos. **County and Themed Books** 128 pages, approximately 150 photos (unless specified). All titles hardback with laminated case and jacket, except those indicated pb (paperback)

Amersham, Chesham & Rickmansworth (pb)	1-85937-340-2	£9.99	Devon (pb)	1-85937-297-x	£9.99
Andover (pb)	1-85937-292-9	£9.99	Devon Churches (pb)	1-85937-250-3	£9.99
Aylesbury (pb)	1-85937-227-9	£9.99	Dorchester (pb)	1-85937-307-0	£9.99
Barnstaple (pb)	1-85937-300-3	£9.99	Dorset (pb)	1-85937-269-4	£9.99
Basildon Living Memories (pb)	1-85937-515-4	£9.99	Dorset Coast (pb)	1-85937-299-6	£9.99
Bath (pb)	1-85937-419-0	£9.99	Dorset Living Memories (pb)	1-85937-584-7	£9.99
Bedford (pb)	1-85937-205-8	£9.99	Down the Severn (pb)	1-85937-560-x	£9.99
Bedfordshire Living Memories	1-85937-513-8	£14.99	Down The Thames (pb)	1-85937-278-3	£9.99
Belfast (pb)	1-85937-303-8	£9.99	Down the Trent	1-85937-311-9	£14.99
Berkshire (pb)	1-85937-191-4	£9.99	East Anglia (pb)	1-85937-265-1	£9.99
Berkshire Churches	1-85937-170-1	£17.99	East Grinstead (pb)	1-85937-138-8	£9.99
Berkshire Living Memories	1-85937-332-1	£14.99	East London	1-85937-080-2	£14.99
Black Country	1-85937-497-2	£12.99	East Sussex	1-85937-606-1	£9.99
Blackpool (pb)	1-85937-393-3	£9.99	Eastbourne (pb)	1-85937-399-2	£9.99
Bognor Regis (pb)	1-85937-431-x	£9.99	Edinburgh (pb)	1-85937-193-0	£8.99
Bournemouth (pb)	1-85937-545-6	£9.99	England In The 1880s	1-85937-331-3	£17.99
Bradford (pb)	1-85937-204-x	£9.99	Essex - Second Selection	1-85937-456-5	£14.99
Bridgend (pb)	1-85937-386-0	£7.99	Essex (pb)	1-85937-270-8	£9.99
Bridgwater (pb)	1-85937-305-4	£9.99	Essex Coast	1-85937-342-9	£14.99
Bridport (pb)	1-85937-327-5	£9.99	Essex Living Memories	1-85937-490-5	£14.99
Brighton (pb)	1-85937-192-2	£8.99	Exeter	1-85937-539-1	£9.99
Bristol (pb)	1-85937-264-3	£9.99	Exmoor (pb)	1-85937-608-8	£9.99
British Life A Century Ago (pb)	1-85937-213-9	£9.99	Falmouth (pb)	1-85937-594-4	£9.99
Buckinghamshire (pb)	1-85937-200-7	£9.99	Folkestone (pb)	1-85937-124-8	£9.99
Camberley (pb)	1-85937-222-8	£9.99	Frome (pb)	1-85937-317-8	£9.99
Cambridge (pb)	1-85937-422-0	£9.99	Glamorgan	1-85937-488-3	£14.99
Cambridgeshire (pb)	1-85937-420-4	£9.99	Glasgow (pb)	1-85937-190-6	£9.99
Cambridgeshire Villages	1-85937-523-5	£14.99	Glastonbury (pb)	1-85937-338-0	£7.99
Canals And Waterways (pb)	1-85937-291-0	£9.99	Gloucester (pb)	1-85937-232-5	£9.99
Canterbury Cathedral (pb)	1-85937-179-5	£9.99	Gloucestershire (pb)	1-85937-561-8	£9.99
Cardiff (pb)	1-85937-093-4	£9.99	Great Yarmouth (pb)	1-85937-426-3	£9.99
Carmarthenshire (pb)	1-85937-604-5	£9.99	Greater Manchester (pb)	1-85937-266-x	£9.99
Chelmsford (pb)	1-85937-310-0	£9.99	Guildford (pb)	1-85937-410-7	£9.99
Cheltenham (pb)	1-85937-095-0	£9.99	Hampshire (pb)	1-85937-279-1	£9.99
Cheshire (pb)	1-85937-271-6	£9.99	Harrogate (pb)	1-85937-423-9	£9.99
Chester (pb)	1-85937-382 8	£9.99	Hastings and Bexhill (pb)	1-85937-131-0	£9.99
Chesterfield (pb)	1-85937-378-x	£9.99	Heart of Lancashire (pb)	1-85937-197-3	£9.99
Chichester (pb)	1-85937-228-7	£9.99	Helston (pb)	1-85937-214-7	£9.99
Churches of East Cornwall (pb)	1-85937-249-x	£9.99	Hereford (pb)	1-85937-175-2	£9.99
Churches of Hampshire (pb)	1-85937-207-4	£9.99	Herefordshire (pb)	1-85937-567-7	£9.99
Cinque Ports & Two Ancient Towns	1-85937-492-1	£14.99	Herefordshire Living Memories	1-85937-514-6	£14.99
Colchester (pb)	1-85937-188-4	£8.99	Hertfordshire (pb)	1-85937-247-3	£9.99
Cornwall (pb)	1-85937-229-5	£9.99	Horsham (pb)	1-85937-432-8	£9.99
Cornwall Living Memories	1-85937-248-1	£14.99	Humberside (pb)	1-85937-605-3	£9.99
Cotswolds (pb)	1-85937-230-9	£9.99	Hythe, Romney Marsh, Ashford (pb)	1-85937-256-2	£9.99
Cotswolds Living Memories	1-85937-255-4	£14.99	Ipswich (pb)	1-85937-424-7	£9.99
County Durham (pb)	1-85937-398-4	£9.99	Isle of Man (pb)	1-85937-268-6	£9.99
Croydon Living Memories (pb)	1-85937-162-0	£9.99	Isle of Wight (pb)	1-85937-429-8	£9.99
Cumbria (pb)	1-85937-621-5	£9.99	Isle of Wight Living Memories	1-85937-304-6	£14.99
Derby (pb)	1-85937-367-4	£9.99	Kent (pb)	1-85937-189-2	£9.99
Derbyshire (pb)	1-85937-196-5	£9.99	Kent Living Memories(pb)	1-85937-401-8	£9.99
Derbyshire Living Memories	1-85937-330-5	£14.99	Kings Lynn (pb)	1-85937-334-8	£9.99

Available from your local bookshop or from the publisher

Frith Book Co Titles (continued)

Title	ISBN	Price	Title	ISBN	Price
Lake District (pb)	1-85937-275-9	£9.99	Sherborne (pb)	1-85937-301-1	£9.99
Lancashire Living Memories	1-85937-335-6	£14.99	Shrewsbury (pb)	1-85937-325-9	£9.99
Lancaster, Morecambe, Heysham (pb)	1-85937-233-3	£9.99	Shropshire (pb)	1-85937-326-7	£9.99
Leeds (pb)	1-85937-202-3	£9.99	Shropshire Living Memories	1-85937-643-6	£14.99
Leicester (pb)	1-85937-381-x	£9.99	Somerset	1-85937-153-1	£14.99
Leicestershire & Rutland Living Memories	1-85937-500-6	£12.99	South Devon Coast	1-85937-107-8	£14.99
Leicestershire (pb)	1-85937-185-x	£9.99	South Devon Living Memories (pb)	1-85937-609-6	£9.99
Lighthouses	1-85937-257-0	£9.99	South East London (pb)	1-85937-263-5	£9.99
Lincoln (pb)	1-85937-380-1	£9.99	South Somerset	1-85937-318-6	£14.99
Lincolnshire (pb)	1-85937-433-6	£9.99	South Wales	1-85937-519-7	£14.99
Liverpool and Merseyside (pb)	1-85937-234-1	£9.99	Southampton (pb)	1-85937-427-1	£9.99
London (pb)	1-85937-183-3	£9.99	Southend (pb)	1-85937-313-5	£9.99
London Living Memories	1-85937-454-9	£14.99	Southport (pb)	1-85937-425-5	£9.99
Ludlow (pb)	1-85937-176-0	£9.99	St Albans (pb)	1-85937-341-0	£9.99
Luton (pb)	1-85937-235-x	£9.99	St Ives (pb)	1-85937-415-8	£9.99
Maidenhead (pb)	1-85937-339-9	£9.99	Stafford Living Memories (pb)	1-85937-503-0	£9.99
Maidstone (pb)	1-85937-391-7	£9.99	Staffordshire (pb)	1-85937-308-9	£9.99
Manchester (pb)	1-85937-198-1	£9.99	Stourbridge (pb)	1-85937-530-8	£9.99
Marlborough (pb)	1-85937-336-4	£9.99	Stratford upon Avon (pb)	1-85937-388-7	£9.99
Middlesex	1-85937-158-2	£14.99	Suffolk (pb)	1-85937-221-x	£9.99
Monmouthshire	1-85937-532-4	£14.99	Suffolk Coast (pb)	1-85937-610-x	£9.99
New Forest (pb)	1-85937-390-9	£9.99	Surrey (pb)	1-85937-240-6	£9.99
Newark (pb)	1-85937-366-6	£9.99	Surrey Living Memories	1-85937-328-3	£14.99
Newport, Wales (pb)	1-85937-258-9	£9.99	Sussex (pb)	1-85937-184-1	£9.99
Newquay (pb)	1-85937-421-2	£9.99	Sutton (pb)	1-85937-337-2	£9.99
Norfolk (pb)	1-85937-195-7	£9.99	Swansea (pb)	1-85937-167-1	£9.99
Norfolk Broads	1-85937-486-7	£14.99	Taunton (pb)	1-85937-314-3	£9.99
Norfolk Living Memories (pb)	1-85937-402-6	£9.99	Tees Valley & Cleveland (pb)	1-85937-623-1	£9.99
North Buckinghamshire	1-85937-626-6	£14.99	Teignmouth (pb)	1-85937-370-4	£7.99
North Devon Living Memories	1-85937-261-9	£14.99	Thanet (pb)	1-85937-116-7	£9.99
North Hertfordshire	1-85937-547-2	£14.99	Tiverton (pb)	1-85937-178-7	£9.99
North London (pb)	1-85937-403-4	£9.99	Torbay (pb)	1-85937-597-9	£9.99
North Somerset	1-85937-302-x	£14.99	Truro (pb)	1-85937-598-7	£9.99
North Wales (pb)	1-85937-298-8	£9.99	Victorian & Edwardian Dorset	1-85937-254-6	£14.99
North Yorkshire (pb)	1-85937-236-8	£9.99	Victorian & Edwardian Kent (pb)	1-85937-624-X	£9.99
Northamptonshire Living Memories	1-85937-529-4	£14.99	Victorian & Edwardian Maritime Album (pb)	1-85937-622-3	£9.99
Northamptonshire	1-85937-150-7	£14.99	Victorian and Edwardian Sussex (pb)	1-85937-625-8	£9.99
Northumberland Tyne & Wear (pb)	1-85937-281-3	£9.99	Villages of Devon (pb)	1-85937-293-7	£9.99
Northumberland	1-85937-522-7	£14.99	Villages of Kent (pb)	1-85937-294-5	£9.99
Norwich (pb)	1-85937-194-9	£8.99	Villages of Sussex (pb)	1-85937-295-3	£9.99
Nottingham (pb)	1-85937-324-0	£9.99	Warrington (pb)	1-85937-507-3	£9.99
Nottinghamshire (pb)	1-85937-187-6	£9.99	Warwick (pb)	1-85937-518-9	£9.99
Oxford (pb)	1-85937-411-5	£9.99	Warwickshire (pb)	1-85937-203-1	£9.99
Oxfordshire (pb)	1-85937-430-1	£9.99	Welsh Castles (pb)	1-85937-322-4	£9.99
Oxfordshire Living Memories	1-85937-525-1	£14.99	West Midlands (pb)	1-85937-289-9	£9.99
Paignton (pb)	1-85937-374-7	£7.99	West Sussex (pb)	1-85937-607-x	£9.99
Peak District (pb)	1-85937-280-5	£9.99	West Yorkshire (pb)	1-85937-201-5	£9.99
Pembrokeshire	1-85937-262-7	£14.99	Weston Super Mare (pb)	1-85937-306-2	£9.99
Penzance (pb)	1-85937-595-2	£9.99	Weymouth (pb)	1-85937-209-0	£9.99
Peterborough (pb)	1-85937-219-8	£9.99	Wiltshire (pb)	1-85937-277-5	£9.99
Picturesque Harbours	1-85937-208-2	£14.99	Wiltshire Churches (pb)	1-85937-171-x	£9.99
Piers	1-85937-237-6	£17.99	Wiltshire Living Memories (pb)	1-85937-396-8	£9.99
Plymouth (pb)	1-85937-389-5	£9.99	Winchester (pb)	1-85937-428-x	£9.99
Poole & Sandbanks (pb)	1-85937-251-1	£9.99	Windsor (pb)	1-85937-333-x	£9.99
Preston (pb)	1-85937-212-0	£9.99	Wokingham & Bracknell (pb)	1-85937-329-1	£9.99
Reading (pb)	1-85937-238-4	£9.99	Woodbridge (pb)	1-85937-498-0	£9.99
Redhill to Reigate (pb)	1-85937-596-0	£9.99	Worcester (pb)	1-85937-165-5	£9.99
Ringwood (pb)	1-85937-384-4	£7.99	Worcestershire Living Memories	1-85937-489-1	£14.99
Romford (pb)	1-85937-319-4	£9.99	Worcestershire	1-85937-152-3	£14.99
Royal Tunbridge Wells (pb)	1-85937-504-9	£9.99	York (pb)	1-85937-199-x	£9.99
Salisbury (pb)	1-85937-239-2	£9.99	Yorkshire (pb)	1-85937-186-8	£9.99
Scarborough (pb)	1-85937-379-8	£9.99	Yorkshire Coastal Memories	1-85937-506-5	£14.99
Sevenoaks and Tonbridge (pb)	1-85937-392-5	£9.99	Yorkshire Dales	1-85937-502-2	£14.99
Sheffield & South Yorks (pb)	1-85937-267-8	£9.99	Yorkshire Living Memories (pb)	1-85937-397-6	£9.99

See Frith books on the internet at www.francisfrith.co.uk

FRITH PRODUCTS & SERVICES

Francis Frith would doubtless be pleased to know that the pioneering publishing venture he started in 1860 still continues today. Over a hundred and forty years later, The Francis Frith Collection continues in the same innovative tradition and is now one of the foremost publishers of vintage photographs in the world. Some of the current activities include:

Interior Decoration

Today Frith's photographs can be seen framed and as giant wall murals in thousands of pubs, restaurants, hotels, banks, retail stores and other public buildings throughout the country. In every case they enhance the unique local atmosphere of the places they depict and provide reminders of gentler days in an increasingly busy and frenetic world.

Product Promotions

Frith products are used by many major companies to promote the sales of their own products or to reinforce their own history and heritage. Frith promotions have been used by Hovis bread, Courage beers, Scots Porage Oats, Colman's mustard, Cadbury's foods, Mellow Birds coffee, Dunhill pipe tobacco, Guinness, and Bulmer's Cider.

Genealogy and Family History

As the interest in family history and roots grows world-wide, more and more people are turning to Frith's photographs of Great Britain for images of the towns, villages and streets where their ancestors lived; and, of course, photographs of the churches and chapels where their ancestors were christened, married and buried are an essential part of every genealogy tree and family album.

Frith Products

All Frith photographs are available Framed or just as Mounted Prints and Posters (size 23 x 16 inches). These may be ordered from the address below. From time to time other products - Address Books, Calendars, Table Mats, etc - are available.

The Internet

Already fifty thousand Frith photographs can be viewed and purchased on the internet through the Frith websites and a myriad of partner sites.

For more detailed information on Frith companies and products, look at these sites:

www.francisfrith.co.uk
www.francisfrith.com
(for North American visitors)

See the complete list of Frith Books at:

www.francisfrith.co.uk

This web site is regularly updated with the latest list of publications from the Frith Book Company. If you wish to buy books relating to another part of the country that your local bookshop does not stock, you may purchase on-line.

For further information, trade, or author enquiries please contact us at the address below:
The Francis Frith Collection, Frith's Barn, Teffont, Salisbury, Wiltshire, England SP3 5QP.
Tel: +44 (0)1722 716 376 Fax: +44 (0)1722 716 881 Email: sales@francisfrith.co.uk

---

See Frith books on the internet at www.francisfrith.co.uk

HOW TO ORDER YOUR FREE MOUNTED PRINT
and other Frith prints at half price

Mounted Print
Overall size 14 x 11 inches

Fill in and cut out this voucher and return it with your remittance for £2.25 (to cover postage and handling to UK addresses). For overseas addresses please include £4.00 post and handling.
Choose any photograph included in this book. Your SEPIA print will be A4 in size. It will be mounted in a cream mount with a burgundy rule line (overall size 14 x 11 inches).

Order additional Mounted Prints at HALF PRICE (only £7.49 each*)

If you would like to order more Frith prints from this book, possibly as gifts for friends and family, you can buy them at half price (with no additional postage and handling costs).

Have your Mounted Prints framed

For an extra £14.95 per print* you can have your mounted print(s) framed in an elegant polished wood and gilt moulding, overall size 16 x 13 inches (no additional postage and handling required).

---

* IMPORTANT!

These special prices are only available if you order at the same time as you order your free mounted print. You must use the ORIGINAL VOUCHER on this page (no copies permitted). We can only despatch to one address.

Voucher for **FREE** and Reduced Price Frith Prints

Please do not photocopy this voucher. Only the original is valid, so please fill it in, cut it out and return it to us with your order.

Picture ref no	Page number	Qty	Mounted @ £7.49	Framed + £14.95	Total Cost
		1	Free of charge*	£	£
			£7.49	£	£
			£7.49	£	£
			£7.49	£	£
			£7.49	£	£
			£7.49	£	£
Please allow 28 days for delivery			* Post & handling (UK)		£2.25
			Total Order Cost		£

Title of this book . . . .

I enclose a cheque/postal order for £ . . . .
made payable to 'The Francis Frith Collection'

OR please debit my Mastercard / Visa / Switch / Amex card
(credit cards please on all overseas orders), details below

Card Number

Issue No (Switch only)   Valid from (Amex/Switch)

Expires   Signature

Name Mr/Mrs/Ms ....

Address ....

....

....

.... Postcode ....

Daytime Tel No ....

Email ....

Valid to 31/12/05

Send completed Voucher form to:
The Francis Frith Collection, Frith's Barn, Teffont, Salisbury, Wiltshire SP3 5QP

Would you like to find out more about Francis Frith?

We have recently recruited some entertaining speakers who are happy to visit local groups, clubs and societies to give an illustrated talk documenting Frith's travels and photographs. If you are a member of such a group and are interested in hosting a presentation, we would love to hear from you.

Our speakers bring with them a small selection of our local town and county books, together with sample prints. They are happy to take orders. A small proportion of the order value is donated to the group who have hosted the presentation. The talks are therefore an excellent way of fundraising for small groups and societies.

Can you help us with information about any of the Frith photographs in this book?

We are gradually compiling an historical record for each of the photographs in the Frith archive. It is always fascinating to find out the names of the people shown in the pictures, as well as insights into the shops, buildings and other features depicted.

If you recognize anyone in the photographs in this book, or if you have information not already included in the author's caption, do let us know. We would love to hear from you, and will try to publish it in future books or articles.

Our production team

Frith books are produced by a small dedicated team at offices in the converted Grade II listed 18th-century barn at Teffont near Salisbury, illustrated above. Most have worked with the Frith Collection for many years. All have in common one quality: they have a passion for the Frith Collection. The team is constantly expanding, but currently includes:

Jason Buck, John Buck, Douglas Burns, Ruth Butler, Heather Crisp, Isobel Hall, Hazel Heaton, Peter Horne, James Kinnear, Tina Leary, Sue Molloy, Hannah Marsh, Kate Rotondetto, Dean Scource, Eliza Sackett, Terence Sackett, Sandra Sanger, Lewis Taylor, and Shelley Tolcher.